reci ...
wk

M000216818

15.85

WHAT THE **BIBLE** TEACHES ABOUT

CHRISTIAN PARENTING

Roger Ellsworth

EVANGELICAL PRESS

EVANGELICAL PRESS
Faverdale North, Darlington, DL3 0PH, England

e-mail: sales@evangelicalpress.org

Evangelical Press USA
P. O. Box 825, Webster, New York 14580, USA

e-mail: usa.sales@evangelicalpress.org

web: http://www.evangelicalpress.org

© Roger Ellsworth 2007. All rights reserved. No part of this publication may be reproduced, stored in a retrieval system or transmitted, in any form, or by any means, electronic, mechanical, photocopying, recording or otherwise, without the prior permission of the publishers.

First published 2007

British Library Cataloguing in Publication Data available

ISBN-13   978-0-85234-648-8   ISBN 0-85234-648-4

All Scripture quotations, unless otherwise indicated, are taken from the New King James Version. Copyright © 1988 by Thomas Nelson, Inc. Used by permission. All rights reserved.

Printed and bound in the United States of America.

*The following pages are dedicated
to my dear wife Sylvia,
who has consistently modelled
gracious Christian parenting*

Acknowledgements

Once again I am very grateful to David Clark and Bob Dickie for encouraging me to participate in the *What the Bible teaches about …* series.

This time the subject was even more formidable and challenging than usual: Christian parenting! I do not think I would have been able to see it through if it had not been for the kind encouragement of my wife Sylvia. I am deeply grateful.

I must also thank my sons Tim and Marty for making my own experience of parenting one of unmingled joy and delight.

And I must also express my appreciation for the valuable assistance of my secretary, Ida Lowery.

May the Lord himself be pleased to use these pages to bring some help and support to my fellow believers who even now are sailing on the exciting sea of parenting.

Contents

Introduction

I remember very well when my two sons were born. What joy and delight there was in gazing into the eyes of those precious little ones!

Yet along with the delight was a heavy sense of responsibility. I was responsible for the well-being of these little boys! Yes, I was responsible for their physical and emotional well-being, but, more importantly, for their spiritual well-being. These were not just temporal little creatures who would live and die. They were beings destined for eternity!

That sense of responsibility became even heavier as I thought about seeking the spiritual welfare of these boys in a society which seemed to put every obstacle possible in the way to my achieving that end.

How could I possibly hope to succeed? And then it came to me! I was not alone in this business! I had been given a guidebook for parenting. No, it was not the new, trendy advice of someone who had discovered a special formula that had eluded former generations. It was in fact a very old book indeed — the Bible!

The Bible, an authority on parenting! Many will regard that as a ridiculous assertion. How can such an old book be considered an authority on any aspect of modern life?

The answer, of course, is that the Bible is no ordinary book. Its teachings are timeless because its author is the eternal God. Yes, men actually wrote the words of the Bible, but they were not left to themselves. They were men whom the Spirit of the Lord inspired to such a degree that the words they wrote were the words of God (2 Timothy 3:16-17; 2 Peter 1:19-21).

Since God himself is always relevant and up-to-date, the Bible will always be the same. An eternally relevant God cannot produce anything but eternally relevant truth.

The Bible is a practical book. It deals with real-life people dealing with real-life problems and seeking real-life solutions. Parenting is one of those areas where many real-life people are finding real-life problems. The Bible has real-life solutions!

Our study of parenting must, therefore, be a study of the Bible. In the pages that follow, we will try to discern what the Bible teaches about Christian parenting.

I should hasten to add that our theme is not 'Christian parenting made easy'. Parenting is not easy! Even with the Bible's teachings in hand, we shall find the task to be challenging. Why is this the case? While the Bible's truth is perfect, Christian parents are far from it. They are not always able to understand what the Bible teaches, and they are not able to perfectly carry out that which they do understand. Their children are not perfect either. Christian parenting amounts to imperfect people seeking to implement perfect truth in the lives of other imperfect people.

A beleaguered mother was asked if she would have children if she could start her life again. 'Sure,' she replied, 'just not the same ones.'

The following comment from a tired father has often been reported: 'I once had no children and six theories on child rearing. I now have six children and no theories on child rearing.'

Child rearing is indeed a formidable task. But there is help in the Bible, and that help comes, not in the form of unproven theories, but rather as guidance that is substantial and true. If we will put its teachings into practice, we will do well in parenting.

Although the task is daunting, we should not despair. The same God who authored the Bible has promised to help us. He gives wisdom (James 1:5) and strength (Isaiah 40:29-31) for every challenge. His grace is sufficient for us (2 Corinthians 12:9).

With the Bible in hand and that hope in our hearts, we can excel — even in the difficult task of parenting.

1. Children are gifts from the Lord

Please read: Psalms 127:3-5; 128:1-4

A familiar couplet says:

Two men looked out from prison bars.
One saw mud, the other stars.

So much of our happiness in life depends on what we choose to look at. It is the same with this matter of parenting. We can look at the mud, or we can look at the stars.

There is quite a bit of mud to be seen in the business of parenting. It is challenging to say the least. Children can be very taxing and trying. But the stars can also be seen. Our children are gifts from the Lord.

The psalms noted at the beginning of this chapter are two of the fifteen 'Songs of Ascents'. These psalms were sung by pilgrims as they made their way to Jerusalem for the great annual festivals. They are called 'Songs of Ascents' because Jerusalem was situated in a mountainous region (Psalm 87:1). To go to Jerusalem, one had to 'ascend'.

The pilgrims also experienced another kind of ascending as they journeyed. The closer they got to Jerusalem, the more their spirits rose with eagerness for the worship that lay ahead and with a sense of blessedness. These festivals were, then, occasions for both physical and spiritual ascent.

The sense of blessedness compelled the authors of these two psalms to think of their families. Let us learn from this that we must not think of blessedness without thinking of our families. In his epistle, James writes: 'Every good gift and every perfect gift is from above, and comes down from the Father of lights, with whom there is no variation or shadow of turning' (James 1:17).

If we call something good, we have to say it is from God! God is the only source of goodness. There is no good to be found in any place except in him. If we consider our children to be good, we must say they come from God. They are his gifts to us.

In this day in which children are so lightly regarded and so casually discarded, Christians must tightly hold and widely proclaim that children are God's good gifts and that parenting is not a burdensome duty but a wondrous privilege. John Benton shares this experience:

> I can remember shopping with my wife in a supermarket and glancing at one of the 'homemaker' magazines which are often available near the check-out. On the front was a headline for an article which read, 'Is there

life after kids?' It reflected a prevalent attitude. Children are the death of joy in marriage. Children are a pain in the neck! There may be many reasons for the world to adopt that view. The expense of children, the attention children require disturb the materialistic, easy life-style. Sometimes children are less than sweet little darlings! But that attitude should never become part of the Christian parents' outlook. If it does, changes need to take place in our homes and in our hearts. The Lord is grieved by such things.[1]

Alun McNabb makes a special appeal to mothers to realize their blessedness:

The task of parenting is heaven-sent. Mothers who are asked, 'Do you have a job?' should never, no never, say 'No.' If you stay at home to look after your children you have the biggest job on earth. Do not be intimidated by those who think otherwise. While some mothers, perhaps out of necessity, go out to 'find' a job, you can know that your job was 'given' to you by God.[2]

Psalms 127 and 128 affirm in a very picturesque way that children are indeed God's gifts to us.

Psalm 127

This psalm is attributed to Solomon, who also authored the book of Ecclesiastes. Solomon packed that book with the word 'vanity', and he begins this psalm with the same thought. It is vain — useless or meaningless — to build a house or guard a city apart from the Lord (v. 1). It is also vain to labour apart from the Lord (v. 2).

With those thoughts in place, Solomon takes up the matter of family life (vv. 3-5). The seeming 'disconnection' between the first two verses and the last three have caused some to suggest that the two sections were originally separate psalms. But that 'disconnection' is in appearance only. There is actually a link here. The purpose of building the house is to provide lodging for a family, and the purpose of guarding the city is to protect the family. The family, then, is not an afterthought or the subject of a separate psalm; it is rather the theme that unifies Psalm 127. It is the thought to which the psalm quite naturally progresses.

The point is that children are such good gifts from the Lord that they make our other endeavours worthwhile. And the other point is that we can no more rear children without God's help than we can build a house or guard a city!

We can no more rear children without God's help than we can build a house or guard a city!

Having made this connection, Solomon affirms that children are a 'heritage' from the Lord. Back in the days of Joshua, the people of Israel received a 'heritage' in the land of Canaan. Lots were cast, and land was apportioned. Solomon wanted his readers to understand that just as that land was God's gift to their forefathers, so their children were his gifts to them.

Children are also God's 'reward' (v. 3). Albert Barnes says of children: '…they are among the blessings which God promises, and are evidences of his favor'.[3]

Solomon also likens children to arrows. The children given by God grow up to protect us in our old age! So the man is 'happy' who has a full quiver (v. 5). By the way, as Warren Wiersbe observes, our children can also be 'arrows for fighting the Lord's battles, so keep them polished and sharp and aimed in the right direction'.[4]

Solomon brings his psalm to a conclusion by declaring the value of children 'in the gate'. The gate of the city was the place where a great deal of business was conducted and even where litigation took place. A man could expect his children to grow into adults who would look out for his best interests.

Psalm 128

This psalm, whose author is unidentified, also sounds the note of children as gifts from the Lord. The author conveys this by calling them 'olive plants' around the table (v. 3). James Montgomery Boice offers this explanation:

Olive trees take a long time to mature and become profitable. Patiently cultivated, they become quite valuable and continue to produce a profitable crop for centuries, longer perhaps than any other fruit-producing tree or plant.[5]

And patiently cultivated children will continue to bring blessing! Albert Barnes adds:

17

Look upon this picture. See the farmer cultivating his fields; see him gathering in the grain; see him at his own table calmly, quietly, and gratefully enjoying the fruit of his toil. Look upon that picture of a happy family — numerous, cheerful, beloved — giving promise of upholding the name of the family in future years — and see all this as coming from the Lord — and you have an illustration of the blessedness which follows a religious life.[6]

Are children good gifts? Ask the ancient Israelite if he considered his allotment of land to be good. Ask the ancient warrior if he considered arrows to be good. Ask the ancient farmer if a flourishing olive tree was good. You have your answer. Children are blessings from God.

A mother had sons who liked to play in the garden, and she had bare ground to show for it. When asked why she didn't stop her boys from ruining the grass, she replied: 'You can always grow grass, but you can't always grow little boys.'

She knew her blessedness.

Remember this …

1. *The way in which we choose to look at the task of parenting has much to do with our success.*

2. *The Bible teaches us to regard our children as gifts from the Lord that have the potential to bring great blessing into our lives.*

2. The goal is godliness

Please read: Malachi 2:15; Ephesians 6:4

In the comic strip 'Peanuts', we sometimes find Snoopy aspiring to write a novel. He always starts with the same words: 'It was a dark and stormy night.'

On one such occasion, Lucy comes along, reads what he has written and immediately rebukes him: 'You stupid beagle! Don't you know anything? Every story begins with "Once upon a time". You stupid beagle!'

With that she walks away, leaving Snoopy to ponder her words. After doing so, he types: 'Once upon a time, it was a dark and stormy night.'

I wonder if future authors might write of our time: 'Once upon a time, it was a dark and stormy night for the family.'

We can rest assured that each generation has had its difficulties with the rearing of children, but ours seems to have as much or more trouble than any previous generation.

Someone has offered this shrewd bit of wisdom: If you aim at nothing, you will probably hit it! A good part of the family's 'dark and stormy night' is undoubtedly due to parents not knowing what they are aiming at.

It is frighteningly possible to hit nothing with our children. We can produce zeroes, and the likelihood of doing so increases dramatically if we do not go about parenting with the right goal in mind.

Many parents over the last several years have perceived their goal to be that of instilling high self-esteem in their children. This approach is bound to produce people who are self-centred and go through life with a sense of entitlement; that is, with the idea that they are entitled to receive whatever they want without concern for anyone else. In recent years, some school administrators and teachers have begun to question how healthy our society can be if we continue to promote individual self-esteem.

Other parents have goals that they refuse to admit. Some, for example, seek to recapture their own youth through their children. It is as if these parents want to go to high school again! They want their teenagers to be popular. Perhaps the parents themselves were popular and want to now relive that time through their youngsters. Or it could be that the parents were not popular in school, and they now want their children to achieve that which they could not.

While non-Christians may very well have either no goals or the wrong goals in their parenting, there should be no confusion among Christians about the matter. It is stated so very clearly in the texts cited above. The goal is to produce 'godly offspring' (Malachi 2:15). It is to bring our children up in 'the training and admonition of the Lord' (Ephesians 6:4). The word 'training' (some translations have 'discipline') is more general and refers to every kind of instruction. The word 'admonition' (sometimes translated 'instruction') puts the emphasis on the training provided through speaking. To put it another way, 'training' emphasizes more the general conduct of the parents, while 'admonition' points more to the speaking of the parents.

There should be no confusion among Christians about the matter ... The goal is to produce 'godly offspring'.

However, the key thing is the phrase 'of the Lord'. The parents, and particularly the father, are by their general conduct and specific verbal messages to direct the children in the way of the Lord.

Dr Martyn Lloyd-Jones provides this admirable summary of the apostle Paul's teaching in Ephesians 6:4:

Children are to be reared in 'the nurture and the admonition' — and then the most important addition of all — 'of the Lord': 'the nurture and admonition of the Lord'. This is where Christian parents, engaged in their duty towards their children, are in an entirely different category from all other parents. In other words, this appeal to Christian parents is not simply to exhort them to bring up their children in terms of general morality or good manners or commendable behaviour in general. That, of course, is included; everyone should be doing it; non-Christian parents should be doing it.

They should be concerned about good manners, good general behaviour, an avoidance of evil; they should teach their children to be honest, dutiful, respectful, and all these various things. That is but common morality, and Christianity has not started at that point. Even pagan writers interested in the good ordering of society have always exhorted their fellow-men to teach such principles. Society cannot continue with a modicum of discipline and of law and order, at every level, and at every age. But the Apostle is not referring to that only; he says that the children of Christians are to be brought up 'in the nurture and admonition of the Lord'.

It is at this point that the peculiar and specific Christian thinking and teaching enter. In the forefront of the minds of Christian parents must ever be the thought that the children are to be brought up in the knowledge of the Lord Jesus Christ as Saviour and as Lord. That is the peculiar task to which Christian parents alone are called. This is not only their supreme task; their greatest desire and ambition for their children should be that they should come to know the Lord Jesus Christ as their Saviour and as their Lord.[1]

The goal is godliness! Yes, Christian parents join non-Christians parents in wanting their children to be happy, healthy and successful. And, yes, it is okay for us to desire that they have the right kind of self-esteem, but Christians understand that these goals, praiseworthy as they are, do not rise to the level of the supreme goal of godliness. Christian parents also understand that the lesser goals are tied to the higher.

While Christian parents use such terms as 'our children' or 'my children', they know that the truth of the matter is that children are ours only in a secondary way. Primarily, our children are a 'trust'. We understand what it means to hold something in 'trust'. It means we have been given responsibility for property owned by another, and we are to administer that property in keeping with what the owner wants.

Children are God's property. They belong to him, and he has given parents the responsibility of administering them according to what he wants. What does God want to see in those children? Godliness!

Remember this …

1. *By their general conduct and by their speaking, parents are to direct their children in the Lord's way.*

2. *Our children belong to the Lord, and parents are stewards who hold them in trust for him.*

3. Two important questions

Please read: Psalm 1; Isaiah 57:20-21; 1 Timothy 6:6

I say it again — the goal in Christian parenting is godliness. God wants Christian parents to produce 'godly offspring'. He wants Christian parents to bring their children up in 'the training and admonition of the Lord'.

Parents want their children to be happy. But what produces happiness? That is the key. Many parents think it is produced by allowing their children to do whatever they want. Parents cannot say 'No' because that would make their children unhappy! Incredibly enough, lots of parents, in the name of their children's happiness, are allowing those children to uncritically accept destructive thinking, to company with destructive people and to engage in destructive behaviour! Where is the wisdom in all of that?

It is very important for us to identify godliness as the goal of Christian parenting, but merely identifying it is not enough.

We must also be able to answer two vital questions about the matter.

What is godliness?

One thing we can say for sure is that godliness is the opposite or reverse of godlessness, which is that approach to life that excludes any thought of God or reference to him as the law-giver and rightful ruler to whom we must eventually give account.

The godly person cannot live without reference to God. It is true, of course, that the godly person came into this world in exactly the same way as the godless person. We all come in the same way, that is, with a nature that is opposed to God (Ephesians 2:1-3). But the godly person has not been left to himself. Yes, he came into this world in a state of spiritual deadness. He was dead toward God. But in mercy and grace, God made him alive. And having been made alive, he suddenly understood that he had been made by God and that he was destined to meet God. And he understood that he was not prepared for this meeting; that, as a sinner, he could not stand acceptably in the presence of the holy God. But this same grace also enabled him to see that the Lord Jesus Christ lived and died for the express purpose of enabling sinners to be saved from their sins.

The godly person is one who realizes that he is not a product of chance but rather was created by God in the image of God with the responsibility and privilege of living for the honour of God. He is, then, one who has been saved from sin and condemnation and given title to eternal glory. Now the godly person cannot live as if that never happened! He cannot live without reference to God. The cry of his redeemed heart is the same as that of Saul of Tarsus: 'Lord, what do you want me to do?' (Acts 9:6).

The godly person is one who seeks to live in such a way as to reflect the traits and character of God. He seeks to live in such a way that others can see God in him. He wants to live in such a way that he will bring honour and glory to God. He is profoundly aware that he was made to glorify God and enjoy him for ever.

The godly person recognizes that God is indeed his rightful ruler, and that he, the godly person, must live in conformity to God's laws.

The godly person lives with a God-consciousness. He cannot help but view all of life in terms of God and his revealed Word.

The godly person views God as his resource and stay, and resorts to him and gravitates toward him in every situation and with every problem.

What is godliness? It is knowing God, loving God, reflecting God and living for God. And, yes, even children and teenagers are required by God to live this way. If a child professes to be a believer in Christ, but does not exhibit the traits of godliness, there is every reason to be concerned about his or her spiritual condition. Tedd Tripp summarizes:

> No wonder we lose our kids. We lose them because we fail to think clearly about man's chief end. The chief end of man is to glorify God and to enjoy Him for ever; therefore, your objective in every context must be to set

a biblical world-view before your children. From their earliest days, they must be taught that they are creatures made in the image of God — made for God. They must learn that they will only 'find themselves' as they find Him. Your child must grow to see that real living is experienced when he stands before God and says, 'Whom have I in heaven but you? And being with you I desire nothing on earth' (Psalm 73:25).[1]

Is it good to be godly?

The devil is one grand liar, and one of his most successful lies is that godliness brings misery and woe while sinfulness brings happiness and joy. Satan has long enjoyed linking godliness with being dour and sour. He loves to portray the godly person as one who cannot enjoy himself and is afraid that someone somewhere might be doing just that.

Some time ago I asked a group of teenagers to tell me what they considered to be the very worst thing that anyone could say about them. Their answer? To be called a 'goody-goody'.

As I probed further, I discovered that a 'goody-goody' is someone who simply tries to do the right thing. It is someone who respects authority and who lives according to the rules! As far as these young people were concerned, it was not good to be good.

I found myself wondering what they would have said about godliness, which involves more than mere human goodness.

Godliness is often misrepresented these days, but it is a good thing. The prevailing notion is that it destroys our happiness. The truth is it secures it.

Godliness is not the enemy of happiness but its true, unfailing friend.

There is certainly nothing wrong with parents seeking the happiness of their children. All parents should! But let us make sure that we understand that godliness is not the enemy of happiness but its true, unfailing friend. In other words, let's be sure that we understand the devil's lie to be exactly what it is — a lie! We parents must work consistently and diligently to convince our children of this.

Stop and think about it for a moment: if we were made by God to live for God, doesn't it make sense to say that we cannot find happiness apart from God?

It is no accident that the Bible so frequently connects godliness with blessedness or happiness. A prime example is found in Psalm 1, which begins with an exultant burst: 'Blessed is the man...' This amounts to the psalmist saying: 'How very happy is the man...'

It would seem to many that the author of this psalm was setting off on a fool's errand. Imagine it! The man intends to show that the person who devotes himself to living a godly and righteous life is the one who finds true happiness! And the one who lives without regard to God is the miserable person!

The world has it the other way. The God-devoted person is miserable! And those who live unshackled by thoughts of God find the fun!

Time will prove the psalmist to be correct. And time will also prove Isaiah to be correct. He says 'the wicked are like the troubled sea' (Isaiah 57:20).

This is the flip side of Psalm 1. There we have the godly person compared to a tree that is firmly planted. It is sending out beautiful boughs. It is clothed in beautiful foliage and is laden with fruit. But according to Isaiah, the godless person does not have the stability and serenity of that tree. He or she is more like the churning sea. There is no real peace or happiness in godless living.

To be good parents, we must go to school on this matter of godliness. We must study it diligently. That is the key. If we want to spare our children all kinds of heartache, grief and turbulence, we must be convinced that godliness is our goal and go after it with all our hearts.

Christian parents understand that godliness must be their goal in parenting. There is:

- no heaven apart from godliness (Hebrews 12:14);
- no real happiness apart from godliness (Isaiah 57:20-21);
- no benefit for society apart from godliness (Proverbs 14:34; 29:2).

With these things firmly fixed in their minds, Christian parents know that they must do all they can to lead their children to faith in Christ, and, once those children have come to Christ, do all they can to promote their growth as Christians.

Going after godliness in our children! What a wonderful and high goal! We can look at parenting as a risky process that we have to get through, or we can look at it as an exciting adventure in which we link arms with God to accomplish something for eternity.

J. C. Ryle offers these wise words to parents:

Beware of that miserable delusion into which some have fallen — that parents can do nothing for their children; that you must leave them alone, wait for grace, and sit still. These persons have wishes for their children in Balaam's fashion — they would like them to die the death of the righteous man, but they do nothing to make them live his life. They desire much, and have nothing. And the devil rejoices to see such reasoning, just as he always does over anything which seems to excuse indolence, or to encourage neglect of means.[2]

Much of our success in parenting hinges on the perspective we choose to adopt. This truth is pointedly made by the old story of three men who were digging. When asked what they were doing, the first said he was digging a ditch, the second that he was earning a living and the third that he was building a house.

Parenting is a drudgery if we see it as digging a ditch and a delight if we see it as building a house. And the house is godliness!

Remember this …

1. *Godliness means knowing, loving, reflecting and living for God.*

2. *Godliness does not destroy happiness, but rather secures it.*

31

4. The gap and the bridge

Please read: Psalms 51:5; 58:3; Romans 1:1-17

If godliness is our goal in parenting, how big is our task? Here is another way to put it: how wide is the gap between our children and our goal? Is the gap relatively small and easily bridged? Are our children already inclined towards godliness? Do they need only a little help in this direction?

The Bible leaves no doubt about the answers to such questions. The gap between our children and godliness is exceedingly wide. Humanly speaking, it is an unbridgeable chasm.

How we perceive the nature of the material we are working with — our children — will determine how we go about the task of parenting. If we believe that children are basically good and that parents can only mess them up ('There are no bad kids, only bad parents'), we will be continually hesitant and filled with doubt and guilt. If, on the other hand, we accept the

Bible's teaching about our children, we position ourselves to channel the good news of its grace to them.

The Bible is a very realistic book. It tells us the truth about ourselves no matter how uncomfortable it makes us. When it comes to parenting, the Bible will not allow us to don rose-coloured glasses. It plainly affirms that each person comes into this world with a sinful nature. That includes our children!

The gap

In the two psalms mentioned above, King David of Israel affirms the sinfulness of human nature.

Psalm 51:5

David knew the truth about himself. He had committed extremely vile and wicked sins: an adulterous liaison with Bathsheba, a treacherous plot to have her husband killed and a prolonged period in which he refused to admit his sin and repent! The sad story is laid out in sickening detail in 2 Samuel 11:1 - 12:23.

Psalm 51 is his prayer of heartfelt repentance. After trying to cover his sinful deeds for months, David is now looking in every crevice to discover sin. He wants it all set out in the noonday sun. As he ponders it all, David realizes that it is not sufficient for him to confess the sinfulness of his acts. He must also confess the sinfulness of his nature. His wrong deeds flowed from a wrong nature. He does not offer this as an excuse but only states it as a fact.

Psalm 58:3

◇◇◇◇◇◇◇◇◇◇◇◇◇◇◇◇◇◇◇◇◇◇

The Bible is a very realistic book. It tells us the truth about ourselves no matter how uncomfortable it makes us.

◇◇◇◇◇◇◇◇◇◇◇◇◇◇◇◇◇◇◇◇◇◇

This verse is about leaders who refuse to defend the people of God. Citizens have the right to expect justice from their magistrates, but when David took up his pen to write, justice had not been carried out. The problem was in their hearts. They could not be right in their judgements because they were wrong in their hearts.

David leaves us in no doubt about the root of the problem. The wicked are wicked because they are born wicked. They come into this world with a sinful nature that manifests itself in both their mouths and their ears. They speak words that are deceitful and harmful (v. 3), and they refuse to listen to words of correction. In both cases, they are like snakes! In their speaking, they resemble the poisonous viper who injects its venom. In their refusal to hear, they are just like the deaf cobra that cannot be charmed no matter how alluring the music.

Christian parents know about the sinful nature of their children because it is taught in the Bible. But they also know it from their children. We are not far into the process of parenting before we hear our children saying a defiant 'No!' or a selfish 'Mine!'

The innate sinfulness of our children is proven by the fact that we never have to teach them to do wrong. They incline toward it! But we constantly have to teach them to do right. We never have to teach them to lie, but we must work diligently to

35

get them to tell the truth. We never have to teach them to lose their tempers, but we must vigorously teach them to control their anger.

So Christian parents approach their task with keen awareness of a vast gap between their goal of godliness and the reality of the godless nature of their children.

The bridge

If our children are to be godly, they must first experience a change that only God can provide. They must receive from God a new nature that inclines them towards godliness. Parents cannot produce this. They can pray for it, speak to their children about it and put them under the teaching and preaching of God's Word. But the work is finally God's.

The good news is that God does this work. Are our children spiritually dead? God stops by the spiritual cemetery and gives life to dead sinners! (Ephesians 2:1-4). The apostle Paul, who so firmly and graphically portrayed the deadness of sinners, gloriously writes: 'But God, who is rich in mercy, because of his great love with which he loved us, even when we were dead in trespasses, made us alive together with Christ (by grace you have been saved), and raised us up together and made us sit together in the heavenly places in Christ Jesus...' (2:4-6).

God's saving work flows from his heart of love

The apostle gloried in God's 'great love with which he loved us'. The sinner is one who refuses to acknowledge God as his

Creator and his rightful sovereign. He refuses to live according to God's laws.

The Lord would be completely justified in bringing judgement upon such rebellious creatures, but, wonder of wonders, he loves sinners.

Who can begin to comprehend the glory and marvel of what God has done for his people? He has granted them life, raised them up and given them fellowship with himself.

The apostle John was astonished at the love of God, writing: 'Behold what manner of love the Father has bestowed on us, that we should be called children of God!' (1 John 3:1).

The words 'what manner' is translated from a Greek phrase which means 'from what country'. John was familiar with various kinds of love, but the love of God for sinners was different from anything he had known. He had nothing with which to compare it. It was utterly foreign to him.

The best loved verse in the Bible affirms this love: 'For God so loved the world that he gave his only begotten Son, that whosoever believes in him should not perish but have everlasting life' (John 3:16). Anyone who has thought deeply about the love of God cannot help but join Frederick M. Lehman in singing:

> The love of God is greater far
> Than tongue or pen can ever tell;
> It goes beyond the highest star,
> And reaches to the lowest hell…
>
> Could we with ink the ocean fill,
> And were the skies of parchment made;

Were every stalk on earth a quill,
And every man a scribe by trade;
To write the love of God above
Would drain the ocean dry;
Nor could the scroll contain the whole,
Though stretched from sky to sky.

God's saving love flows through Christ

We must not for one moment think that God's love for sinners means that he disregards their sins. God cannot ignore sin. His holy nature will not allow him to do so. That holy nature requires him to pronounce sentence upon sin, and God has pronounced that sentence, namely, eternal separation from himself. The sentence makes perfect sense. Since God's holiness will not allow him to fellowship with sinners in heaven, those sinners must be driven from his presence for ever (Acts 17:30-31; Romans 14:12; 2 Thessalonians 1:9-10; Hebrews 9:27; 1 Peter 4:5; Revelation 21:27).

We can speak, then, of God's tremendous dilemma. On one hand, his holy justice demanded that the sentence against sinners be carried out. On the other hand, his loving nature demanded that he find a way to admit sinners into his presence.

How could God at one and the same time judge and forgive sinners? How could he satisfy the demands of both his justice and his love?

The answer is found in the Lord Jesus Christ. Jesus came to this earth in our humanity to perform a very precise and important mission. He came to satisfy God's justice against sinners and to provide the way for those sinners to be forgiven.

He did so by dying on the cross. There he received the wrath of God in the place of sinners. Yes, eternity was compressed upon him! He actually endured an eternity's amount of wrath in the place of all who will believe on his name. That is why he cried: 'My God, my God, why have you forsaken me?' (Matthew 27:46).

He went to hell on the cross. He bore there the hell of his people. And God's justice, seeing that the penalty was carried out, was satisfied. Now here is the glory of it all: justice only demanded that the penalty for sin be paid once, and if Jesus paid it on behalf of sinners, those same sinners do not have to pay it themselves.

That which Jesus did for sinners made it possible for God to be both just (carrying out his sentence against sinners) and the justifier of sinners (pronouncing them guiltless).

> When Satan tempts me to despair,
> And tells me of the guilt within,
> Upward I look, and see him there
> Who made an end of all my sin.
> Because the sinless Saviour died,
> My sinful soul is counted free;
> For God, the just, is satisfied
> To look on him and pardon me.
>
> (Charitie Bancroft)

So both justice and mercy looked upon the cross with satisfaction; justice because its penalty was carried out, and mercy because believing sinners are set free. The following Scriptures show us something of the nature of Jesus' death on the cross: Isaiah 53:4-12; Romans 3:24-26; 2 Corinthians 5:19-21; Hebrews 2:17; 1 Peter 2:21-24; 3:18; 1 John 4:10.

The basis, then, on which God grants life to spiritually dead sinners is the death of Jesus on their behalf.

God's saving work is received by faith

How does the work of Christ come to apply to us? It is through faith. And what is faith? It is receiving what Christ has done. Our salvation is provided by grace, but it is received by faith. We might say the hands of grace are the working hands in salvation while the hands of faith are merely the receiving hands. God works and we receive, and God works even to this degree — that the faith with which we receive salvation is given to us by him (Ephesians 2:8).

> Believing parents cannot help but hold the gospel ... before their children as the only ... way for them to stand ... in the presence of God.

Those who have been saved by the gospel cannot help but be passionate about the gospel, and believing parents cannot help but hold the gospel constantly before their children as the only possible way for them to stand acceptably in the presence of God.

J. C. Ryle urges parents to keep uppermost in their minds the salvation of their children: 'No interest should weigh with you so much as their eternal

40

interests. No part of them should be so dear to you as that part which will never die.'[1]

Remember this …

1. *Our children are born with a sinful nature, which makes the gap between them and God incredibly wide.*

2. *God grants salvation to sinners on the basis of the redeeming work of Jesus on the cross.*

5. The Word of God

Please read: Psalm 119:1-3,9,38; 2 Peter 1:16-21

Even after our children have been visited by the saving work of God, they are still a long way from godliness. When we are blessed with a baby, we understand that he or she is a real human being but far from being mature. It is the same with God's family. While we are born into his family through salvation, we are far from being mature. Salvation does not perfect us in this life. That will come when God finally calls us into his own presence.

This is the reason the apostle Peter says we must with all diligence 'add' to our faith (2 Peter 1:5-8). Christians do not come full grown!

While Christian parents, then, are filled with gratitude that God has savingly worked in their children, they must also understand that they, the parents, must still work for the godliness of their children. How are they to do this?

I have learned through bitter experience that it is impossible to do certain jobs if I do not use the right tools. I remember trying to change an oil filter on my car several years ago. I made no progress at all until I secured the proper tool. With that tool in hand, the difficult task became easy.

While the task of parenting will never be easy, it is certainly made more so by using the tools God has appointed for the task.

The goal is godliness! We cannot produce it in ourselves, let alone in our children, but the God who has appointed godliness as the end for Christian parenting has also appointed certain means to the end. One of these is God's Word, the Bible. Is the Bible really an essential tool in seeking the godliness of our children? Consider Psalm 119:9:

How can a young man cleanse his way?
By taking heed according to your word.

Consider also Psalm 119:38 as translated in the New American Standard Bible:

Establish Thy word to Thy servant,
As that which produces reverence for Thee.

Why is the Bible a tool for godliness? Because it is the Word of God! It is his revealed truth. God is the expert on godliness, and he has given us all we need to know about the matter in his Word.

The apostle Peter explains the Word of God in this way: '...no prophecy of Scripture is of any private interpretation, for prophecy never came by the will of man, but holy men of God spoke as they were moved by the Holy Spirit' (2 Peter 1:20-21).

> God is the expert on godliness, and he has given us all we need to know about the matter in his Word.

His word 'moved' is very interesting. It means 'carried along'. Here is a man out on the lake in his boat. He hoists the sail, and the wind catches it and drives the boat along the surface of the lake.

We have the Bible because the Holy Spirit of God took men of God and carried or drove them along. They were not left to themselves! They were so carried along by the Holy Spirit that they wrote what he wanted them to write.

Because the Bible is divine in its origin, it is sufficient for us. The apostle Peter describes Scripture as 'a light that shines in a dark place' (2 Peter 1:19).

The dark place is this world. Now there are different degrees of darkness, but the word that Peter uses refers to dark darkness. It is the darkness of a mine or cellar. This darkness is such that it is impossible for us to find our way without a light. But there is a light shining. It is the Word of God. And it tells us why the world is as dark as it is and how to walk in this dark world. It is our guide to godliness!

But the surest guide is of no value if it is not followed. So the apostle Peter tells us that we 'do well to heed' the Word of God. We must give it careful and close attention, and we must lovingly encourage our children to do the same. We must ever be putting the Word of God in their way, urging them as we do so to read, study and apply it, to meditate on it and to memorize it, to discuss it with others and to listen to it preached and taught.

With regard to parents bringing the Bible to their children, J. C. Ryle writes: 'Fill their minds with Scripture. Let the Word dwell in them richly. Give them the Bible, the whole Bible, even while they are young.'[1]

Remember this …

1. *The Bible is a tool for achieving godliness because it is the Word of God.*

2. *We cannot expect the Bible to produce godliness in our children if we do not put its teachings before them.*

6. Utilizing the Word of God

Please read: Deuteronomy 6:1-9; 11:13-25

The Bible as a tool for promoting godliness is plainly set before us in the words the Lord spoke to the people of Israel in Deuteronomy 6:6-9:

> And these words which I command you today shall be in your heart. You shall teach them diligently to your children, and shall talk of them when you sit in your house, when you walk by the way, when you lie down, and when you rise up. You shall bind them as a sign on your hand, and they shall be as frontlets between your eyes. You shall write them on the doorposts of your house and on your gates.

These words create a warm and touching scene: Dad and Mum talking to their children about what is truly important and valuable as they journey along the road of life together. Driving the children to school, sitting down to eat, watching a television programme — in every situation and circumstance, the welfare of the child and the wonderful things of God are never far from the Christian parent's mind. And he takes up every opportunity to bring the child and the truth together.

I have to say that my father was a master at turning our family farm into a school. He would carry a New Testament in the chest pocket of his overalls. And as we worked, we talked, and as we talked the conversation would inevitably lead to him producing that New Testament. Out it would come and into it we would go! It was all so natural. He had no more trouble talking about it than he did the weather. The impression was that it was part of his life — the main part — and that it should be the same with me.

I shall never forget him stepping up to the cardboard that he had nailed to the inside of the barn walls (to keep at bay the frightful blasts of winter wind), taking out his pencil and sketching out his understanding of the description of the heavenly city (Revelation 21 & 22). He spoke about it with such wonder! Well, I never forgot it. That may very well have been the day when God put heaven into my heart and stamped eternity on my eyeballs.

Years later, when he died, I journeyed back to be with my family for his funeral. I wondered if those sketchings were still there. And they were! Time had made the lines very faint but the hope more vivid and real.

The way many Christians go about the work of parenting leaves a far different impression — like working in a factory. The time clock is punched, the machines are whirring, the product is going down the assembly line, the whistle blows, the clock is punched again and the day is over.

If we take this rigid, mechanical approach to parenting, we fall short of the biblical ideal. The Christian is to be a fruit tree that naturally produces fruit. He is not to be a Christmas tree. His Christianity is to be an integral part of him, not something that is external only.

The spirit with which we do all this is crucial. If we go about it with a sense of heaviness, as if we are only seeking

> If our children can see that the things of God are delightful to us … we will achieve much.

to discharge an unpleasant duty, we will achieve very little. But if our children can see that the things of God are delightful to us, that we are talking out of hearts that have been touched by the grace of God, we will achieve much.

The working of Christianity into the fabric of everyday life means that we must bring the teaching of the Bible to bear on every area of life. We must talk about life, about what we read in the newspaper and see on television. The opportunities to identify harmful and destructive thoughts and behaviour are plentiful. We must seize them, explaining why such things are wrong and how to avoid them.

As our children get older, we must make it our business to discuss social and moral issues with them from the biblical world view, never failing to challenge the erroneous assumptions and conclusions that are so prevalent in society. We must ask our children what they think about a particular idea. Is it true or not? Is that action right or wrong?

We do our children a great service if we help them to think critically about those things with which they are confronted instead of accepting them at face value. Throughout the course of a day, several opportunities will present themselves for this kind of discussion.

We must really listen to our children and always be poised to answer their questions. We must never make them think that we are too busy. A little boy wanted to share something with his father who had his nose stuck in a book. 'Daddy, listen,' he said. The father, book still in front of him, said: 'I'm listening, Son.' But his son said again: 'Daddy, listen.' This time the father, still reading, responded more emphatically: 'I am listening. Go ahead.' And the little boy pulled the book down from his father's face and said: 'Daddy, listen with your eyes.'

One of the very best things we can do for our children is to read to them — especially from the Bible! — when they are very young. The stories of the Bible, which never fail to fascinate children, are a good place to begin.

But let us not be content only to read. Let's discuss what we have read. Ask the children to imagine what it would have been like to have been Joseph — on the way to a strange new world because he was hated and sold by his brothers! What would it have been like to be one of those brothers? Trudging home to lie about Joseph's disappearance! How would it have felt to be in this position?

Ask them to imagine what it would have been like to have been one of the shepherds on the night that Jesus was born.

This kind of discussion helps our children to look more closely at the events reported by Scripture and prompts them to think about the ways in which these events affected ordinary people like themselves.

It is also important for our children to see us reading and studying the Bible. They must be able to see that their parents prize and treasure it as the Word of God. And keep good books on hand for them to read as they grow older. These books can become wonderful opportunities for talking about the things of God.

Let us never forget the importance of leading our children in memorizing God's Word. This can begin when the children are two years old. By the time our children are teenagers, larger passages can be memorized. This can be great fun for the whole family, each member seeking to memorize the verses and taking turns reciting them. This can be done while driving or walking or taking a meal together.

All of this requires great diligence. For years, I have kept a quote posted where my eyes can frequently fall upon it. I do not know the author of these words, but they have certainly helped me to retain my focus: 'In every calling, there must be belief in its great value before there can be intense ardour in its prosecution. It is not in the nature of the mind to be stirred deeply by what it deems a trifle.'

We can only be diligent in our parenting if we believe firmly in the importance of what we are doing.

Translation? We must believe in what we are doing, or we will not be able to do it very well! We can only be diligent in our parenting if we believe firmly in the importance of what we are doing and if we believe that our daily example and conversation are essential elements in us reaching our goals with our children.

Many want good children without having to put in any effort, but we must not separate the means from the end.

Seeing a woman working in her beautiful garden, a man said: 'You certainly have a green thumb.' She responded: 'No, I have a dirty thumb and a purple knee.'[1]

The woman understood the connection between her diligence and her goal — a beautiful garden.

Remember this …

1. *Christian parents should seek to be warm and natural in talking to their children about the Word of God.*

2. *Christian parents must always be looking for opportunities to bring the teachings of the Bible before their children.*

7. The house of God

Please read: Psalm 84

With this term 'the house of God', I am referring to public worship. Do we habitually think of this as one of our primary resources in our efforts to rear godly children? We should. Seeing us delight in public worship will leave an indelible mark on our children.

But why should we delight in public worship? Why should we delight in the house of God and teach our children to do the same?

A God-meeting place

We must answer by saying that it is a God-meeting place. The very fact that the place of worship is called God's house tells us all we need to know. God is there. Yes, God is everywhere, but he is with his people in a special way when they come together for worship.

Nothing is more needful for us when we worship than to be aware that we are in the presence of God. This awareness corrects a thousand wrongs.

A need-meeting place

The house of God is also a need-meeting place. It is a place to find guidance (Psalm 27:4), to hide from the trials and troubles of life (27:5-6) and to have our heads, which have been bowed down with troubles, lifted (27:6).

The house of God is a place for the sparrow (84:3), a common emblem for worthlessness. The devil is quick to assure us that we are such unworthy specimens that God has no use for us and life has no meaning for us. In the house of the Lord, the sparrow finds a home!

The house of God is also a place for the swallow (84:3), a common emblem for restlessness. We search for peace and satisfaction in various places. They are found in the house of God.

A truth-meeting place

The house of God is a truth-meeting place. When Asaph was in trouble on the matter of the wicked prospering while the righteous floundered, he went to the house of God. He writes: 'Then I understood…' (73:17).

Yes, the house of God is a place of understanding. There we hear the Word of God preached and taught. It is our responsibility as parents to expose our children to good Bible teaching and preaching as often as possible. This will certainly involve taking them to the right type of church each Sunday but also taking them to special conferences and events.

It is our responsibility as parents to expose our children to good Bible teaching and preaching as often as possible.

Parents should try to maximize the effect of all such preaching and teaching by talking with their children about what they heard.

But what if we are in a church in which the Word of God is not accurately proclaimed? Saturate the place with your absence!

A family-meeting place

The house of God is also a family-meeting place. We find our brothers and sisters in Christ there. The very fact that they are there helps us. Their presence is a testimony to the truth that God is at work in his world. And we find that they are there to encourage us and help us bear our burdens. Sometimes we are helped by realizing that among those we find there are folks who are far more burdened than we ourselves!

Do our children need these things? Do they need a God-meeting, need-meeting, truth-meeting, family-meeting place?

Of course they do! Let us take them, then, to the house of God! Let us make sure they understand that there is such a thing as the Lord's Day — a day that is to be reserved for the things of God — and that these things are a blessing and privilege.

And — need we say it? — it is very important that we always speak positively and happily about our church and her leaders. Many parents, to their immense and bitter regret, have adult children who will not go to church. The reason? Through their childhood years, they heard their parents complain about various aspects of church life, and they wondered why their parents would give time and attention to something that made them unhappy.

Remember this …

1. *Public worship is a vital part of rearing godly children.*

2. *Parents must display a happy, positive spirit about public worship if they expect their children to prize it.*

8. Personal example

Please read: Philippians 3:17; 4:9

What mighty resources Christian parents have in the Word of God and the house of God! We cannot successfully parent without them.

We have other resources as well. The above verses point us to personal example as a vital resource in fulfilling our awesome task.

Setting a good example in general

The psalmist David points to this resource in these words:

I will behave wisely in a perfect way.
Oh, when will you come to me?
I will walk within my house with a perfect heart
(Psalm 101:2).

David obviously knew the importance of setting the right example. So he resolved to walk within his house 'with a perfect heart'.

No, he was not so full of himself as to think that he was perfect in the sense of being sinless and that he would now put this perfection on display. Albert Barnes understands the phrase 'in a perfect way' to mean 'in accordance with the perfect rules of right', and has the psalmist saying: 'I will make these my guide, I will *aim* to be perfect; I will have before me a perfect standard'[1] (italics are his). The picture is, then, of David setting a good and proper example for his family by seeking to live according to God's perfect requirements.

Christian parents must seek to do the same. We must know that the godliness of our children is our goal in parenting, be convinced of the rightness of that goal and model it for our youngsters. We cannot expect our children to show devotion to God, if we do not show it ourselves. We cannot expect them to show respect to us, if we conduct ourselves in a way that does not deserve respect.

> We cannot expect our children to show devotion to God, if we do not show it ourselves.

Nothing can replace the positive example of parents. Happy parents who love and serve God, who love and respect each other, and who are clean in life and language will most certainly have a powerful impact for good on their children.

How can you lead to Christ your boy
Unless Christ's method you employ?
There's just one thing that you can do —
It's let that boy see Christ in you.

…

The Church that hopes to win the lost
Must pay the one unchanging cost;
She must compel the world to see
In her the Christ of Calvary.[2]

In his letter to Titus, the apostle Paul includes a happy little phrase. In urging Christian slaves to be obedient to their masters, he tells them that by doing so they 'adorn the doctrine of God our Saviour' (Titus 2:9-10). The word 'adorn' means 'to deck or dress with ornaments' or 'to make conspicuous and impressive'.

These slaves had embraced the gospel of Christ. They had been saved from sin and plucked from condemnation by that gospel. The gospel was a beautiful thing. But Paul here asks them to make it more beautiful. He might as well have asked them to wet water, to whiten snow, to warm fire or to brighten a diamond!

It would seem to be an impossible task. But it is not. While the gospel itself is perfect, it does not make us perfect in this life. While we Christians have been forgiven of our sins, we have not been delivered from the possibility of sinning. While its power has been broken in our lives, it still conducts something of a guerilla warfare against us.

As long as the gospel indwells imperfect people, the possibility exists of those people misrepresenting and dishonouring it. Paul wanted Christian slaves to honour it. He wanted them to live in such a winsome and attractive way that they gave credibility to the gospel and made it appealing.

Paul's words to the slaves has application to Christians in every arena of life. It certainly applies to Christian parents. We have in our dealings with our children the opportunity to make our Christianity attractive and appealing or to make it repugnant and repulsive. Alexander Maclaren declares: 'Either you make men think better of God's truth, or you make them think worse of it. There are no worse enemies of the gospel than its inconsistent friends.'[3]

This scathing indictment of the gospel's 'inconsistent friends' was handed down by Mahatma Gandhi: 'There was a time when I wavered between Hinduism and Christianity. When I recovered the balance of my mind, I felt that to me salvation was possible only through the Hindu religion — and my faith in Hinduism grew deeper and more enlightening. But I think I would have become a Christian — if it had not been for Christians.'[4]

Setting a good example in marriage

We must not fail to include in this area the way in which we go about our marriages. Why does God want his people to be faithful to their marriages? Malachi's answer is this: 'He seeks godly offspring' (Malachi 2:15).

God himself is faithful, and he desires for us to be faithful as well. One of the ways we learn faithfulness is by seeing it at work in the home. If God had designed marriage in such a way that a man would not have to be faithful to one woman, the offspring of that marriage would not learn faithfulness. Children determine how they are to relate to others by watching the way in which their parents relate to each other.

Joyce Baldwin writes: 'Only when both parents remain faithful to their marriage vows can the children be given the security which provides the basis for godly living. The family was intended to be the school in which God's way of life was practiced and learned...'[5]

John Benton says of the Lord:

He is seeking godly offspring. He is looking for our children to become disciples. Of course, there is no guarantee that children of Christian parents will automatically embrace the faith of their parents... But we must realize that an unhappy Christian marriage, where the thought life (and therefore probably the words and actions) of the partners is far from perfect harmony, will be a profound obstacle to our children becoming Christians.[6]

Benton further writes:

Our marriages are like a fig tree from which our Lord is expecting fruit. Our marriages are not just for us. They are for the Lord. Does he come to our marriages expecting to find refreshing fruit, but like that fig tree in the Gospels find none, though he had every reason to expect fruit? Why does he find no fruit? Sometimes it is *not* the Christian parents' fault that children rebel. We are all sinners. But sometimes a heavy responsibility for the child's rebellion against the things of God lies with the parents. Sometimes it is the parents' fault. They have brought the name of God into disrepute with the child through what the child has seen in the marriage. This is terribly serious and we should not be surprised that God withdraws[7] (italics are his).

Christian parents must ever realize that they are children themselves — children of God! What is our responsibility as God's children? The apostle Paul answers: '...be followers of God, as dear children' (Ephesians 5:1, AV).

As we do so, we can speak these words to our own children: 'Be ye followers of me, even as I also am of Christ' (1 Corinthians 11:1, AV).

In our general conduct and in our marriages, let us follow Christ, making it our aim as we do to convince our children that the knowledge of Christ is the most wonderful thing in the world.

Remember this ...

1. *Setting the proper example for our children means living according to the commandments of God.*

2. *Christian parents must keep in mind that the example they set in marriage is of particular importance.*

9. Prayer

Please read: Hebrews 4:14-16

If godliness is the goal in child-rearing, prayer is one of our most valuable and effective tools.

Jesus prayed for godliness in the lives of his disciples: 'I do not pray that you should take them out of the world, but that you should keep them from the evil one. They are not of the world, just as I am not of the world. Sanctify them by your truth. Your word is truth' (John 17:15-17).

The apostle Paul also prayed for godliness in the lives of his fellow-believers. He prayed that the saints in Philippi would be 'filled with the fruits of righteousness' (Philippians 1:11). He wrote these words to the believers in Colosse: 'For this reason we also, since the day we heard it, do not cease to pray for you, and to ask that you may be filled with the knowledge of his will in all wisdom and spiritual understanding; that you may walk worthy of the Lord, fully pleasing him, being fruitful in every good work and increasing in the knowledge of God; strengthened with all might, according to his glorious power, for all patience and longsuffering with joy...' (Colossians 1:9-11). Furthermore, Paul prayed that the Thessalonians would have their hearts established 'blameless in holiness' (1 Thessalonians 3:13).

The Bible also gives us an example of the very thing we are talking about, namely, believers praying for the godliness of their children. David prayed for Solomon with these words: 'And give my son Solomon a loyal heart to keep your commandments and your testimonies and your statutes, to do all these things...' (1 Chronicles 29:19).

If God has appointed prayer as one of the means for producing godliness, it is doubtful that we can be effective without it.

Praying for our children

Let us, therefore, pray for our children. Let us pray with gratitude to God, realizing that they are his gifts to us. Let us pray for their salvation, realizing that God alone can awaken, enlighten and save them. Let us pray that they will come to the Lord early in life and that they will bring much glory to him. Let us pray that God will give them much discernment and keep them from evil. Let us pray that God will give them much wisdom regarding the matter of marriage and that he will lead them in this vital area.

I count my parents among my greatest blessings. They were godly people who believed in prayer and practised it. As I went about my chores on our little farm, it was not unusual for me to come upon my father praying. And sometimes I would hear him praying for me. That made a lasting impression!

Praying with our children

While praying for our children is essential, it must not stand alone. We must also pray with them. One of the great losses over recent years is the practice of family worship. And let us pray for ourselves as parents that we will have an abundance of wisdom, grace, strength and patience.

One of the things that will keep us praying is the awareness that we have in the Lord Jesus a High Priest who can 'sympathize with our weaknesses' (Hebrews 4:15).

If two pianos are placed in the same room, a note struck on one will cause the other to gently sound the same note. This is called sympathetic resonance. In like manner, when something strikes the child of God that same chord resonates in the heavenly humanity of Jesus. The point we must understand is not just that it is possible for Jesus to sympathize with us, but rather that it is impossible for him *not* to sympathize with us.

What an encouragement this is for parents as they feel their weaknesses and cry out to the Lord!

> If God has appointed prayer as one of the means for producing godliness, it is doubtful that we can be effective without it.

Teaching our children to pray

While we must most certainly pray for and with our children, we cannot leave it at that. We must also teach them to pray and how to pray.

Every Christian parent feels his inadequacy here! How are we to go about teaching our children to pray? I suggest the 'ACTS' formula.

'A' stands for *adoration*. Prayer properly begins with worship of God. In teaching his disciples to pray, the Lord Jesus began his prayer with these words:

Our Father in heaven,
Hallowed be your name

(Matthew 6:9).

How much there is for us to adore in God! Think of his majesty and splendour, his wisdom, power, justice, holiness, righteousness, faithfulness, unchangeableness, love, mercy and grace. Those who learn to begin prayer with adoration of God inevitably find this to be the best part of prayer, and they will find themselves reluctant to move from it to other things.

The 'C' stands for *confession*. We must pray with the realization that we are very sinful and that our sins impede the flow of our fellowship with God. Confession removes the obstacles and opens the channel (1 John 1:8-9).

The 'T' represents *thanksgiving*. We would think our own children to be very poor if they never expressed gratitude for anything we have done for them, and such ingratitude would make us less inclined to do things for them in the future.

Thanksgiving is no less important in our relationship to God (Philippians 4:6; Colossians 4:2).

The 'S' depicts *supplication*. This is the 'asking' part of prayer in which we present our petitions to God. We are permitted to bring our needs to the Lord with the confidence that he is a caring and wise Father who is ever eager to hear from his children and is pledged to grant what is best for them.

> Thou art coming to a king,
> Large petitions with thee bring;
> For his grace and power are such,
> That no one can ask too much.

We often vex ourselves with the problem of 'unanswered prayer'. The far greater problem is that of 'unasked prayer' (James 4:2). With such a God and such a privilege — the privilege of talking to him — let us make sure that we are praying and encouraging our children to do the same.

Remember this …

1. *Praying for and with our children are vital elements in promoting their godliness.*

2. *The 'ACTS' formula is a good way to teach our children how to pray.*

10. Corrective discipline

Please read: Proverbs 29:17

The word 'discipline' falls into that category of words that has developed a negative and nasty connotation. It is a good word that does not deserve such treatment.

The word in the Old Testament is translated from a Hebrew word (*yasar*) which means 'to instruct, rebuke or warn'. In the New Testament it is translated from a Greek word (*paideuo*), which means 'to instruct or correct'.

It is impossible to move our children towards godliness apart from discipline. But in these topsy-turvy times of muddled thinking and messy living, discipline has come to be regarded as contrary to love.

Just the opposite is true. Discipline expresses the love of the parent for the child, love that is so great that it is willing to take unpleasant action in order to help the child be what he or she ought to be.

Yet discipline need not be unpleasant. As the above definitions indicate, true discipline consists of two parts — the positive and the negative. Or we can think of these two parts as preventive and corrective discipline. The idea behind preventive discipline is to instruct and train the child in such a positive way that he or she will not be inclined to disobey and rebel. The resources we have examined — the Word of God, the house of God, personal example and prayer — may be considered as preventive discipline. The more we succeed in this kind of discipline, the less we will have to practise the corrective discipline.

However, corrective discipline may very well be needed from time to time. This is the type of discipline that requires us to punish for wrongdoing, and punishment itself can consist of withholding privileges from the child or spanking. The latter has come to be regarded in many circles as criminal behaviour, but Christian parents must draw their approach from the Bible, and the Bible says there is a place for it (Proverbs 13:24; 22:15; 23:13; 29:15)!

However, the Word of God also cautions fathers about provoking their children to wrath (Ephesians 6:4; Colossians 3:21). To provoke them means to drive them to the point of exasperation in which they, as it were, throw up their hands in despair. It is to bring them to such a point that they do not know what to say or do.

There are many ways we can bring our children to such a point: always finding fault, never giving praise, being neglectful, unreasonable, inconsistent or verbally and physically abusive. The following lines from Martha Pine illustrate exasperating parenting and contrast it with tender parenting:

Corrective discipline

'I've got two As,' the small boy cried,
His voice was filled with glee.
His father very bluntly asked,
'Why didn't you get three?'

'Mom, I've got the dishes done,'
The girl called from the door.
Her mother very calmly said,
'And did you sweep the floor?'

'I've mowed the grass,' the tall boy said,
'And put the mower away.'
His father asked him with a shrug,
'Did you clean off the clay?'

The children in the house next door
Seemed happy and content.
The same things happened over there,
But this is how it went.

'I've got two As,' the small boy cried,
His voice was filled with glee.
His father proudly said, 'That's great,
I am glad you live with me.'

'Mom, I've got the dishes done,'
The girl called from the door.
Her mother smiled and softly said,
'Each day, I love you more.'

'I've mowed the grass,' the tall boy said,
'And put the mower away,'
His father answered with much joy,
'You've made me happy today.'

Children deserve a little praise,
For tasks they're asked to do.
If they're to lead a happy life,
So much depends on you.

Striving to not provoke our children does not mean we cannot correct them. There is a place for corrective discipline, but it must be carried out with balance and wisdom. What constitutes balanced and wise discipline?

Both parents and children must be very clear on what constitutes wrongdoing

In other words, all must know the rules. And those rules should be communicated early, as well as the reasoning behind them. It is tough on children when parents seem to be making up the rules as the family goes along.

A lady, seeing a little boy struggling to reach a doorbell, lifted him up. After he pushed it several times, the woman asked: 'What now?' He answered: 'Run like crazy!'[1]

Many parents go about their business with the 'What now?' approach. They are not conscious of following a plan to reach a goal. They are reacting instead of acting.

However, the rules should pertain to things that are truly important! How often parents make 'a big deal' out of something that is trivial only to ignore something that is crucial. For example, we should not 'explode' when a child accidentally knocks over a glass of milk, and say nothing when he or she tells a lie or takes God's name in vain.

This point was etched on my mind some years ago when I was sharing a meal with a family. The only son happened to spill his milk, and the father became very angry with him! After delivering a very stern and strong lecture, the father himself knocked a bowl of corn off the table. To his credit, he realized that he had been wrong to scold his child for something that parents can also do.

> It is tough on children when parents seem to be making up the rules as the family goes along.

Discipline should be tailored to the child

The episode of the spilt milk and the upturned corn calls to mind another situation. A sensitive and compliant child overturned his water and immediately began to cry. And the father responded by deliberately spilling his water! A wise man! Children of this type need only a look or word to be corrected. Others require firmer action.

Discipline should also take into account the various stages of the child's development. A punishment that might be fitting for a child of six will not be appropriate for one who is sixteen.

Discipline must always be consistent

Nothing is more exasperating to a child than for rules to constantly be changing. Something is wrong today and okay tomorrow, okay today and wrong tomorrow!

An inconsistent approach often means that we are parenting on the basis of impulse rather than principle. We happen to be irritable and 'stressed' on a particular day, so almost everything the child says or does is wrong. The next day we feel better, and the child's behaviour, although the same as the day before, is now okay.

Dr Martyn Lloyd-Jones observes:

There is nothing more irritating to the one who is undergoing discipline than a feeling that the person who is administering it is capricious and uncertain. There is nothing more annoying to a child than the kind of parent whose moods and actions you can never predict, who is changeable, whose condition is always uncertain. There is no worse type of parent than he who one day, in a kindly mood, is indulgent and allows the child to do almost anything it likes, but who the next day flares up in a rage if the child does scarcely anything at all … Such a parent … fails to exercise a true and helpful discipline, and the position of the child becomes impossible.[2]

A consistent approach also means that we do not threaten punishment without carrying it through.

Yet another aspect of it is that the parents themselves must present a united front to the child. If the father and mother disagree on a matter of discipline, they must work that out privately and not in the presence of the child.

Discipline must never be too severe

We must make sure we are disciplining the child on the basis of principle and not because we are angry. Furthermore, we must explain to the child why the discipline is necessary — not because we're angry and want to get even — but because we want that which is best for him.

We should always be careful how we talk to our children. When the child does something wrong, we should never respond, as some parents do, by saying: 'Can't you do anything right?' That response tells the child that he has not only disappointed you at one point, but that he is *always* a disappointment to you. Dr Lloyd-Jones wisely says:

> ...we must never humiliate another person. If in punishing or administering discipline or correction, we are ever guilty of humiliating the child, it is clear that we ourselves need to be disciplined. Never humiliate! Certainly punish if punishment is called for, but let it be reasonable punishment based upon understanding. And never do it in such a way that the child feels that

he is being trampled upon and being utterly humiliated in your presence, and still more, in the presence of others.[3]

We are Christians because we have been touched by the grace of God, and, as we shall note more fully in the next chapter, we should go about our parenting in such a way as to reflect and display that grace.

Remember this ...

1. *Discipline is one way parents express their love for their children.*

2. *Christian parents must always be clear, understanding, consistent and kind in their dealings with their children.*

11. Parenting like the Father

Please read: Psalm 103

The Bible often refers to God as 'Father'. This was Jesus' favourite term for God (e.g. Matthew 6:9; 7:21; 10:33; 16:17; 26:29,39,42,53; John 5:17,30,43; 15:1,8,10,15).

This is upsetting to some. Many years ago, a lady approached after hearing me preach on the fatherhood of God. I could tell she was angry before she said a word. She soon explained her anger: 'If you had a father like mine, you would never speak about God as Father.'

Many readily identify with this woman. They take no pleasure at all in the fatherhood of God because they associate the teaching with their own cruel, unfeeling fathers. How are we to respond to such people? Surely, the proper thing to say is that those with terrible earthly fathers have more reason to appreciate the fatherhood of God than anyone else. God is nothing at all like fathers who are more like tyrants than fathers.

> To pattern our parenting after God is to manifest to our children the same traits that God manifests towards us.

David's description in the chapter referenced above gives us insight into what God is like and what our parenting will be like if we follow him. God is the perfect father and Christian parents, and particularly fathers, must pattern themselves after him. To pattern our parenting after God is to manifest to our children the same traits that God manifests towards us. We understand, of course, that God is perfect and we are not. We cannot, therefore, perfectly manifest God's traits. But we can strive to do so.

What, then, are God's parenting traits? We could call many passages of Scripture into service here, but Psalm 103 seems to bring out these traits in a wonderful way. It is a powerful affirmation of God's love for his children. That love is displayed in certain ways.

God is merciful and kind towards his children

God is not, as many think, a cruel and harsh tyrant. David writes:

> For as the heavens are high above the earth,
> So great is his mercy toward those who fear him
>
> (v. 11).

Mercy as high as the heavens! That is great mercy!

Do we doubt the mercy of God? We shouldn't. We have evidences of it every day and in every way. Everything that we consider good — family, health, the beauties of creation, friends, food, clothing — comes from the fountain of God's mercy. How shameful that we have the tendency to look right past a thousand blessings, focus on a problem or two and, on that flimsy basis, question the goodness of God!

If the many expressions of God's mercy are not sufficient to squelch our doubt, we can look at the supreme expression of it. That is found at the cross of Christ. Jesus went to that cross to receive the penalty that we deserve for our sins. He was forsaken of God there so that we who believe will never have to be forsaken. Those who truly comprehend the cross never doubt the mercy of God.

Hearts that have been touched by mercy are not at liberty to withhold it from others. Christians are to be kind in all their dealings, and the way in which they deal with their children is no exception. The Lord Jesus says: 'Therefore be merciful, just as your Father also is merciful' (Luke 6:36).

And the apostle Paul writes: 'And be kind to one another, tender-hearted, forgiving one another, even as God in Christ forgave you' (Ephesians 4:32).

J. C. Ryle offers these words to parents:

Love should be the silver thread that runs through all your conduct. Kindness, gentleness, longsuffering, forbearance, patience, sympathy, a willingness to enter into childish troubles, a readiness to take part in childish joys — these are the cords by which a child may be led most easily — these are the clues you must follow if you would find the way to his heart.

Few are to be found, even among grown-up people who are not more easy to draw than to drive.[1]

God is slow to anger with his children

David writes:

> The LORD is merciful and gracious,
> Slow to anger, and abounding in mercy.
> He will not always strive with us,
> Nor will he keep his anger for ever

(v. 8).

Later on, he adds:

> As a father pities his children,
> So the LORD pities those who fear him.
> For he knows our frame;
> He remembers that we are dust

(vv. 13-14).

God is patient and understanding with his children. He does not 'fly off the handle' with them. If we are to pattern ourselves after God, we must be patient and understanding with our children. We must not expect too much too soon from them, especially with regard to godliness.

We must understand that our children are born with a natural animosity towards godliness and will not have a heart for it until they experience the regenerating work of God's grace. Even then, they are still children and need time to mature. Those of us who have been Christians for years still struggle with godliness. We have no right, therefore, to expect our children to advance more rapidly than ourselves. The word 'train' has been translated by some as 'to work patiently'.

Ryle observes:

Children are weak and tender creatures, and, as such, they need patient and considerate treatment. We must handle them delicately, like frail machines, lest by rough fingering we do more harm than good. They are like young plants, and need gentle watering — often, but little at a time.[2]

We must not take God's merciful nature and his slowness to anger to mean that he does not discipline his people. David and the people of Israel could have testified to the contrary!

Many hold the notion that love rules out or cancels discipline. If we love, we must not discipline. If we discipline, we do not love. Tedd Tripp cites a father who said he had to discipline his children because their mother loved them too much to practise discipline.[3]

But this is a false dichotomy. God loves his children and disciplines them, and his discipline is part of his love. So Solomon writes:

> We must not take God's merciful nature and his slowness to anger to mean that he does not discipline his people.

My son, do not despise the chastening of the LORD,
Nor detest his correction;
For whom the LORD loves he corrects,
Just as a father the son in whom he delights

(Proverbs 3:11-12).

God forgives his children

David splendidly says of the Lord:

As far as the east is from the west,
So far has he removed our transgressions from us

(v. 12).

David is telling us that God removes our sins from us to a degree that is incalculable. Think of it like this: if you start journeying north, you will eventually reach the North Pole and then you will start journeying south again. But if you begin journeying east, you always continue going east.

The forgiving nature of God has never been more beautifully depicted than by the Lord Jesus himself in his parable of the prodigal son. The son who had so decisively and harshly turned on his father was finally made to see his folly and make his way home. When the father saw his son approaching, he could have determined to wait until he arrived and stand before him with stony silence and a hard countenance. He could have further determined that the silence would eventually give way to a stern lecture.

But such a strategy was not to be found in the heart of the father. When he saw his son, he 'had compassion, and ran and fell on his neck and kissed him' (Luke 15:20).

Then the father commanded his servants to bring the best robe, a ring and shoes. The robe was a sign of position, the ring a sign of authority and the shoes a mark of a free man. The father was making it clear that he was taking him back as a son.

What we have in the father's reception of his son is the sight of pardoning love. Love that pardons freely! Love that pardons completely! Love that pardons gladly! Love that pardons unreservedly!

That picture of pardoning love must be riveted in the hearts of Christian parents. Our children may do to us very much like this prodigal son did to his father. But we must always remember that we ourselves are nothing but rebels forgiven by our Father. And we must never hold the faults and failings of our children against them.

Remember this …

1. *Patterning our parenting after God means manifesting to our children those traits which God manifests towards us.*

2. *God is always merciful, kind, patient and forgiving with his children.*

12. What about Proverbs 22:6?

Please read: Proverbs 22:6

God's people get more mileage out of some verses of Scripture than they do from others. Psalm 23, John 3:16 and Romans 8:28 come quickly to mind.

When it comes to the matter of parenting, no verse has yielded more mileage than Proverbs 22:6. This is not difficult to understand. Christian parents fervently desire that their children know and serve the Lord. But there are so many things that are stacked against godly parents. We live in a world that thumbs its nose at the things of God and makes ungodly teachings and action very attractive and appealing. There are so many rebellious young people that it appears as if disdain for parents is an inevitable part of growing up. Christian parents, feeling overmatched and outgunned, have turned again and again to Proverbs 22:6.

Many parents have told me over the years that they cling tenaciously to that verse. If it were not for the comfort it gives, they would lose heart. It is indeed a verse that enables Christian parents to have a degree of confidence as they go about their task. Let's examine it.

First, a word about this book of Proverbs! The people of Israel probably made use of proverbs from the earliest years of their history. Part of the covenant responsibility of the people of God was to see to it that their children had proper religious training (Deuteronomy 6:4-9), and in the process of this training they used proverbs.

When King Solomon came to the throne of Israel, there were already a great number of these proverbs in existence. He gathered them into a collection and added several hundred of his own. Some think he also set up special schools for the religious training of young men and that his collection of proverbs was used in those schools.

What are proverbs? Someone has defined them as 'short statements drawn from long experiences'. A proverb is really a verbal shortcut. It comes from the Latin word '*proverba*'. '*Pro*' means 'for', and '*verba*' means 'words'. A proverb then means 'for or in the place of words'.

This particular proverb compels us to think along three lines.

There is a way for children to go

Solomon says parental training should be done with a view to guiding the child 'in the way he should go'. There is disagreement about this phrase. Some maintain that the way to which Solomon was referring is the child's way.

The child's way

This view understands the parent's task to be that of discerning the special abilities and talents of the child and providing the training that will allow him to realize his potential, respecting the child's individuality and interests. F. C. Cook writes: 'The proverb enjoins the closest possible study of each child's temperament and the adaptation of "his way of life" to that.'[1]

G. Campbell Morgan adds:

Every child you have demands special consideration, and solitary attention… You must discover what the child is if you would train that child. I think we have suffered in every way, socially, may I say, politically, and most certainly religiously, by the habit of imagining that we can deal with children in crowds, and treat them all the same way.[2]

No wise parent would disagree with the importance of these observations.

God's way

The other view is that Solomon is referring here to God's way. This view understands him to be saying that every child is expected to walk the same path — the path of devotion to God — and parents are to instruct them accordingly.

> Every child is expected to walk the same path — the path of devotion to God — and parents are to instruct them accordingly.

It is a fact that Solomon devotes much of his attention to describing the ways of foolish and rebellious young people. This means that we should take the way the child should go to be the opposite of the way in which those young people go.

The 'way he should go' is, then, the way of devotion to God, respect and love for parents, and the way of happiness and fulfilment for the child himself. This is the better interpretation.

This way requires training

As we have noticed, the child is not naturally inclined to go God's way. He must be trained or instructed in that way, and that training should be conducted along the lines we have been discussing.

Perhaps all we need to add at this point are the words of the prophet Isaiah:

For precept must be upon precept,
    precept upon precept,
Line upon line, line upon line,
Here a little, there a little

(Isaiah 28:10).

Every day gives us more opportunities to add a little more to helping our children in going God's way, and we must seize each and every one.

J. C. Ryle says to each Christian parent:

I know that you cannot convert your child. I know well that they who are born again are born, not of the will of man, but of God. But I know also that God says expressly, 'Train up a child in the way he should go,' and that He never laid a command on man which he would not give man grace to perform. And I know, too, that our duty is not to stand still and dispute, but to go forward and obey. It is just in going forward that God will meet us. The path of obedience is the way in which He gives the blessing. We have only to do as the servants were commanded at the marriage feast in Cana, to fill the water-pots with water, and we may safely leave it to the Lord to turn that water into wine.[3]

This training will have an unforgettable effect

There is a way for our children to go — God's way — and that way requires careful and diligent training. So far, so good!

Now we come to the troublesome part of the verse:

And when he is old he will not depart from it.

Even with the wise application of training and discipline some children still rebel. It is, sadly enough, possible for godly people to have rebellious children. What are parents to do when this is the case?

Solomon would have us cling mightily to this promise — even though our child may depart for a time and rebel against us, the godly training we have given him will follow him.

> **Even though our child may depart ... and rebel against us, the godly training we have given him will follow him.**

Only if we arm ourselves with this promise can we go about our parenting with confidence.

If you are a parent who has, with all your imperfections and inadequacies, conscientiously tried to train and discipline your child only to see him rebel, hear this word. Don't give up. Continue to love that child. Continue to pray for him, and continue to talk with him or her. In due time that child may very well cease to break your heart and become a source of tremendous pride and consolation.

A professional singer had lived a godless and rebellious life despite having a godly mother. After giving him godly training during his childhood years, she continued to pray for him in his adult years. She died without ever seeing him come to true faith in God. God used her death to cause her son to reflect long and hard on the training and example she had set before him, and he came to faith in Christ. He began closing his concerts by giving testimony to the grace of God that had so wonderfully used his mother.

After wrapping up yet another concert with this testimony, he was approached by a lady who said she would be seeing his mother soon and was wondering if he would like her to deliver a message. The man replied: 'You don't understand. My mother is dead.'

The lady responded: 'I understand very well. Would you like for me to give her a message?'

Then it hit him. The lady was saying that she herself would soon die, and, having the same faith that his mother had, would be seeing her in the presence of the Lord.

So he smiled and said: 'Yes, there is a message I would like for you to deliver. Tell my mother that I will be there.'

Many parents leave this world with no indication that the godly training they gave their children had any effect. But the grace of God is great, and many of these parents will because of that grace find that the very children of whom they despaired will finally 'be there'.

Remember this …

1. *The way for children to go is the way of devotion to God, the way of love and respect for their parents and the way of happiness and fulfilment for themselves.*

2. *Christian parents are responsible to train their children in this way, knowing as they do that their faithful training will make a difference.*

13. Some words for children

Please read: Proverbs 17:21,25; Ephesians 6:1-3

I well remember the days our sons were born as well as the days we brought them home from the hospital. I also remember the joy that my wife and I felt as we embarked upon this new phase of life. And I remember the apprehension I felt. There were all those familiar apprehensions about various sicknesses, the first day of school and so on.

But the greatest apprehension I had was that these little boys that I loved so much might turn out to be rebellious. What if they were to become so wayward that I would lose all the happiness I ever had over them coming into this world and would find myself wishing they had never been born?

That can and does happen. The truth is there are many parents who, if they felt completely free to confess what they feel in their innermost being, would say: 'I wish my child had never been born.'

Their happiness over that child has evaporated and all they feel now is heartache and regret. It may be drinking, drug usage, running with the wrong crowd, filthy language, or sexual immorality. It may be lying and stealing. It may be 'blowing up' at the slightest suggestion of correction or instruction. It may be stubbornly refusing to go to church. Or it may be a combination of all of the above.

Every parent knows the anguish of his own heart.

Words from King Solomon

Knowing that there is no heartache like that of the godly parent who has a wayward child, Solomon appeals to children to listen to the instructions of their parents! (1:8-9; 2:1; 3:1-2; 4:1,20; 5:1; 6:20; 7:1; 13:1; 19:27). He was not content, however, simply to urge children to listen to parents. He also gave them motives or incentives for doing so.

Parents have the child's best interest at heart

Solomon says parental instructions are 'graceful ornaments' on the head (1:9). We should take that to mean that the child who follows his parents' instructions becomes a graceful person who is respected by others. Young people, when your parents give you instructions, please keep this in mind. They do so in order that you might be such a person.

Solomon also says the instructions of parents are 'life' and 'health' (4:22). That can be taken to mean that the child who listens to his parents finds true joy and happiness in this life.

But it also may mean that listening to parental instruction may very well keep one out of an early grave (3:2; 19:16).

Young people, heed this word. Parents are not perfect. They do not know everything (although they do know more than their children!), but they love you more than you will ever know, and their instructions are designed to bring you happiness, not to spoil it.

> [Parental] instructions are designed to bring you happiness, not to spoil it.

That brings us to the second great incentive Solomon uses in his instructions to the young.

Failure to heed parental instruction brings great grief and misery to one's parents (10:1; 15:20; 17:21,25; 19:13)

A rebellious child takes the happiness right out of life for his parents. Every single day they live has a dark cloud hanging over it. There is never a let-up in the heartache they feel. I ask our young people to consider this. Your parents have invested more time, more work, more love and more money in you than you can believe. Do you really want to repay their investment by destroying their happiness?

Failure to heed parental instruction brings a terrible indictment from the Word of God (10:1; 15:5,20; 17:21; 19:13)

Solomon's favourite word for the rebellious child is not very complimentary. He calls him a 'fool'. The fool is one who is insensitive, arrogant and disrespectful. He is one who rejects

95

wise counsel, which, if only heeded, would bring positive benefits into his life. He rejects that which is reasonable to embrace that which is foolish and destructive.

It is easy enough to see many young people in this description! And while it is possible for one to show respect to his parents and still be a fool, it is impossible to show disrespect to them and not be a fool.

Those who want to avoid this indictment, then, must love their parents, listen to their instructions and receive their guidance.

A message from the apostle Paul

When we come to the New Testament, we find more words addressed to children. Paul writes: 'Children, obey your parents in the Lord, for this is right' (Ephesians 6:1).

He then calls their attention to the fifth of the Ten Commandments: 'Honour your father and mother ... that it may be well with you and you may live long on the earth' (Ephesians 6:2-3; Exodus 20:12).

It is interesting that in the midst of his quotation, the apostle interjects these words: 'which is the first commandment with promise'. That comment is somewhat mystifying in light of the fact that this particular commandment is the only one that has a promise attached. Why would Paul say it is the *first* commandment with a promise when it is the only such commandment?

This may have been Paul's way of saying that the commandment has a special quality or uniqueness about it, that it stands out from all the other commandments. How so? For one thing, it is the only commandment that deals with family relationships. And for another thing, it serves as something of a benchmark or indicator of our response to all the other commandments. Christian children who honour their parents must honour the God who gave the parents, and honouring God is the focus of the first four commandments. And children who honour their parents will have little difficulty in respecting the rights of other people, which is the focus of the last five commandments.

What is the promise that is attached to this commandment? Paul answers, 'that it may be well with you and you may live long on the earth' (v. 3). This is not an ironclad guarantee that obedient children will without exception live longer than disobedient children. It is rather to be regarded as a promise that as a general rule those who obey their parents will live longer and better. We can all think of exceptions, such as a child who was obedient, and died. But that does not negate the promise. It is much easier to cite instances of children who met an early death because they were disobedient and rebellious. Generally speaking, the promise is true.

> Christian children who honour their parents must honour the God who gave the parents.

But the main thing on which we are to focus is the nature of the obedience for which Paul calls. He writes: 'Children, obey your parents in the Lord, for this is right' (v. 1). He wants Christian children to view obedience to parents as part of their obedience to the Lord Jesus Christ.

Young people sometimes get the impression that God has a special brand of Christianity for them in which they get all the blessings without having to shoulder the responsibilities. Paul will have none of this. Young people, you are responsible to obey the Lord. You have been saved by the same Lord from the same condemnation and ruin of sin as adults. You have been delivered from the same wrath as they. You must, therefore, love, serve and obey the Lord.

We must go further. Christian young people, you should look upon the matter of obeying your parents as one way the Lord has given you to show the difference that Christianity has made and is making in your life. To do this will not only require that you obey but that you do so with the right spirit. Martyn Lloyd-Jones urges you:

> ...be unlike all other children; ...be unlike those arrogant, aggressive, proud, boastful, evil-speaking children that are round about you at the present time. Show that you are different, show that the Spirit of God is in you, show that you belong to Christ. You have a wonderful opportunity; and it will give Him great joy and great pleasure.[1]

Christian young people, the Lord Jesus who saved you is also your example in this area as he is in every other area of life. Luke's Gospel tells us that Jesus 'was subject' to his parents (Luke 2:51). Please follow his example by obeying your parents so that you will never have to look back on your childhood years with bitter regret. In my years as a pastor, I have heard many express regret that they treated their parents with disrespect. I have never heard anyone express regret for showing respect to his parents.

Remember this ...

1. *Children should realize that their parents have their best interests at heart, and they should make it their goal to never deliberately engage in behaviour that will break the hearts of their parents.*

2. *Christian children must view obedience to their parents as one aspect of their obedience to the Lord Jesus Christ.*

14. Godly parenting in ungodly times

Please read: 1 Samuel 1:19 - 2:11

Hannah is making her way down the dusty road from Ramath Zophim to Shiloh. With her are her husband Elkanah and her young son Samuel.

The tabernacle of the Lord was at Shiloh, as were Eli, the high priest, and his sons. The ark of the covenant was also there. Hannah and Elkanah had been to Shiloh many times for the various religious festivals conducted there, but this trip was different. Hannah had made a special vow to the Lord that Samuel would be devoted to the Lord's service all of his life, and the time had now come for her and Elkanah to leave their young son with Eli at the tabernacle.

Two great tides of emotions must have slammed against each another in Hannah as she walked along that day. Great gratitude welled up within her as she thought about what the Lord had done for her. When it looked like she was destined to be childless, the Lord had heard her prayer and given her and her husband their precious son. She did not have to make a special commitment of Samuel to the Lord. It wasn't something the Lord required of her, but the heart of sincere love and gratitude always desires to do more than what is required. So it was with Hannah. Her special commitment was the tangible way she found to express her thanksgiving to the God who had so stunningly blessed her.

But the tide of gratitude no sooner reached its peak than another tide rolled up to slam against it — a tide of pain over the thought of separation from her beloved son and uncertainty about what lay ahead of him.

The searing reality of separating would have been difficult enough. Few things in life are more difficult than being separated from those who are near and dear to us. All of us who have laid loved ones to rest know the sharp thrust of that dagger.

Yet the pain of separation was coupled with an uncertainty about the future. These were not good days in Israel. Moral laxity abounded on every hand. It seemed for all the world that responsibility and discipline had fallen to the ground to be swept away with the trash and rubbish. The laws of God were treated as mere ancient relics that had no meaning or usefulness. The general tone and tenor of that day was for each person to make up his own laws as he went along.

Why would the tattered moral fibre of Israel be of concern to Hannah as she trudged along the path to Shiloh? It would seem that the best thing she could do to protect her son from the onslaught of moral permissiveness was what she and her husband were doing. What better place for Samuel to be protected from evil and nurtured in the things of God than at the tabernacle of God?

But, alas, the moral decline had reached even into the very tabernacle of God and tainted the priests. Hophni and Phinehas, the sons of Eli, were depraved and immoral specimens, who were greedy for gain and sexual conquests (2:12-17,22). Eli himself was untainted by the black cloud of immorality that hung over Israel, but he was a very weak man who could only raise a feeble protest against the conduct of his sons.

Furthermore, these things were known throughout the nation of Israel. The scandalous behaviour of Hophni and Phinehas and the weakness and timidity of Eli were both written large before the eyes of the people of Israel.

Hannah must have wondered if she and her husband were doing the right thing in following through on their commitment and leaving Samuel at the very tabernacle where wickedness and weakness abounded. They seemed to be taking their young son into the very teeth of the storm. How could he turn out to be godly in the midst of such circumstances?

Christian parents identify with these things. We know what it is to feel the swelling tide of uncertainty over the future of our children rise up around us. We also live in trying times, times of moral laxity and confusion, times when God's laws are scorned and disdained, times in which people make up their

> We live in trying times ... when God's laws are scorned and disdained, [when] people make up their own rules as they go along.

own rules as they go along. Yes, our times have even seen wickedness and moral weakness reach all the way into the professional ministry.

All of this makes the rearing of godly children extremely difficult and challenging. Sometimes it seems impossible. All the different aspects of our society seem to have come together in a gigantic conspiracy to undermine the morality of our children, and Christian parents do not know how to respond. We know we cannot keep our children from the moral contamination of our day by locking them up and throwing away the key. But what can we do?

Hannah can help us. She knew all about the floodtide of wickedness in Israel and at the tabernacle. She knew all about the pathetic weakness of Eli. But she also knew some other things — things that can help us raise our children in fearful times.

We will now look at two certainties that she held on to: the sufficiency of God, and his ultimate victory over evil.

The present sufficiency of God for his people

Look at her prayer in the opening verses of chapter two and you will find only a hint or two about the evil circumstances of that day but a great deal about God. Eight times we find the phrase 'the Lord'. Once we find the phrase 'the Lord's'. Fourteen times we find Hannah using a pronoun for God. That makes a total of twenty-three times that Hannah makes mention of God in a prayer that takes up only ten verses.

We can say, therefore, that Hannah may have glanced at her circumstances, but she gazed at her God. I fear many of us have reversed this pattern. We gaze at our problems and circumstances and we glance at God. What we gaze at is what occupies our minds and what occupies our minds is what governs and controls our lives. If we gaze at our problems we will constantly feel overwhelmed and overmatched, but if we gaze at God we will find the resources we need for facing the challenges of life.

What did Hannah see as she gazed at God? She saw his power to deliver and preserve his people. Hannah had experienced this power herself. Her situation had looked utterly bleak and hopeless, but God had intervened and given her a child. She begins her prayer by celebrating this deliverance. 'I rejoice in your salvation,' she says (v. 1). In this context, the word salvation refers to God freeing or delivering his people from any situation of crisis or danger.

A little later, Hannah celebrates the great power of God by saying: 'there is none besides you, nor is there any rock like our God' (v. 2). We associate rocks with strength, and God is, according to Hannah, a rock like no other. In other words, he is unrivalled in strength.

Hannah knew that this powerful God who had been at work in her life would be at work in the life of her son. She was taking young Samuel into a situation so difficult that it looked like it would be impossible for him to turn out right, but God's strength was sufficient for that situation.

Sometimes it seems to us that the power of evil is so great that everything that is nailed down is going to come loose and that the very earth itself will be destroyed. Hannah took refuge in the knowledge that God has securely established this earth (v. 8), and that nothing can destroy it until he himself brings it to its appointed end. When the whole world seems to be tottering from the great power of evil, rest in this — the strength of sin is great, but the strength of God is greater.

Furthermore, Hannah took refuge in the knowledge that God can guard the steps of his people even while they walk in this wicked world (v. 9).

The future victory of God over all evil

'No one is holy like the Lord,' says Hannah (v. 2). Then she goes on to say: 'For the Lord is the God of knowledge; and by him actions are weighed.'

The latter statement tells us that God knows all about evil. None of it has escaped his notice. He has seen it all. The former statement tells us he is not ambivalent or neutral about evil. God's holiness means he is not only untainted by evil himself, but that he has sworn eternal hostility against it. God's holiness guarantees that he will finally judge all evildoers and will eliminate all evil.

God's holiness guarantees that he will finally judge all evildoers and will eliminate all evil.

This truth was powerfully manifested in Israel in Samuel's early years. Evil flourished for a long time, and the people no doubt thought they were getting away with it; but God suddenly moved in judgement to sharply curtail it and to bring the people back to a state of spiritual vitality. The judgements God uses to curtail evil in this world simply foreshadow the final judgement in which 'the adversaries of the LORD shall be broken in pieces' (v. 10), and 'the wicked shall be silent in darkness' (v. 9).

There are, then, two great truths to sustain the people of God in evil times. One is that God is the preserver of his people in evil times. He will guard their steps until their work here is done, and he will then take them home to heaven where they shall be so perfectly preserved that nothing will be able to touch them again. The other truth is that God is the great leveller. Evil may flourish so much that it appears to have triumphed, but God is going to level it to the ground. He is sworn to bring evildoers low and to lift his people high.

The best thing Christian parents can do for their children in these evil days is to hold before them these truths. We should labour to make sure they understand the greatness of God. We should labour to help them see that God preserves his people. We should labour to help them grasp the truth that God sees evil and will judge it. It essentially comes down to this: if we parents are to do well in rearing our children we must remember great men and great women have great parents, and great parents have a great God.

Remember this ...

1. *While Christian parenting is always difficult, it is even more so in times of abounding wickedness and apostasy.*

2. *In difficult times, Christian parents can take refuge in both the present sufficiency and the future victory of God.*

Notes

Chapter 1 – Children are gifts

1. John Benton, *Losing Touch with the Living God*, Evangelical Press, p.133.
2. Alun McNabb, 'Children and discipline', *Evangelical Times*, October 1999, p.13.
3. Albert Barnes, *Barnes Notes: Psalms*, Baker Books, vol. iii, p.251.
4. Warren Wiersbe, *With the Word*, Oliver Nelson Publishers, p.398.
5. James Montgomery Boice, *Psalms*, Baker Books, vol. iii, p.1128.
6. Barnes, *Psalms*, vol. iii, p.254.

Chapter 2 – The goal is godliness

1. D. Martyn Lloyd-Jones, *Life in the Spirit*, Baker Book House, pp.291-2.

Chapter 3 – Two important questions

1. Tedd Tripp, *Shepherding a Child's Heart*, Shepherd Press, p.48.
2. J. C. Ryle, *The Upper Room*, The Banner of Truth Trust, pp.288-9.

Chapter 4 – The gap and the bridge

1. Ryle, *The Upper Room*, p.289.

Chapter 5 – The Word of God

1. Ryle, *The Upper Room*, p.292.

Chapter 6 – Utilizing the Word of God

1. Brian L. Harbour, *From Cover to Cover*, Broadman Press, p.246.

Chapter 8 – Personal example

1. Barnes, *Psalms*, vol. iii, p.59.
2. The words of this unknown author are cited by William Hendriksen, *New Testament Commentary: John*, vol. ii, p.254.
3. Alexander Maclaren, *Expositions of Holy Scripture*, Baker Book House, vol. xv, p.135.
4. R. G. Lee, *By Christ Compelled*, Zondervan Publishing House, pp.37-8.
5. Joyce G. Baldwin, *Haggai, Zechariah, Malachi*, Inter-Varsity Press, pp.240-1.
6. Benton, *Losing Touch*, p.79.
7. As above, p.80.

Chapter 10 – Corrective discipline
1. Harbour, *From Cover to Cover*, p.226.
2. Lloyd-Jones, *Life in the Spirit*, pp.279-80.
3. As above, p.283.

Chapter 11 – Parenting like the Father
1. Ryle, *The Upper Room*, p.285.
2. As above, p.286.
3. Tripp, *Shepherding*, pp.37-8.

Chapter 12 – What about Proverbs 22:6?
1. F. C. Cook, *Barnes Notes: Proverbs to Ezekiel*, Baker Books, p.62.
2. bibleteacher.org: sermons by G. Campbell Morgan, 'The Training of Our Children', pp.4-5.
3. Ryle, *The Upper Room*, p.289.

Chapter 13 – Some words for children
1. Lloyd-Jones, *Life in the Spirit*, p.248.

Resources for Christian parents to use with their children

A book for family worship — Jim Cromarty
A year in the Bible with your children — Jim Cromarty
Bible Wise (series) — Christian Focus Publications
Big Thoughts for Little Thinkers — Joey Allen
Big Truths for Little Kids — Susan and Richie Hunt
Books for family reading (series) — Jim Cromarty
Caught in the web — Faith Cook
Learn about God (series) — Christian Focus Publications
Old Paths for Little Feet — Carol Brandt
The Big Picture Story Bible — David Helm
The Picture Bible — Chariot Victor Publishing
The Picture Bible — Cook Communications Ministries
Truth and Grace Memory Book — Thomas K. Ascol (Ed.)
Under the scaffold — Faith Cook
365 Bible Stories for Young Hearts — Crossway Books

Day One Publications and P & R Publishing also publish a range of helpful books especially for children and young people.

WHAT THE **BIBLE** TEACHES ABOUT

CHRISTIAN PARENTING